Chinese Pioneering Inventions Series

Karez Well

Edited by Li Chaodong
Translated by Xuemeng Angela Li

Books Beyond Boundaries
ROYAL COLLINS

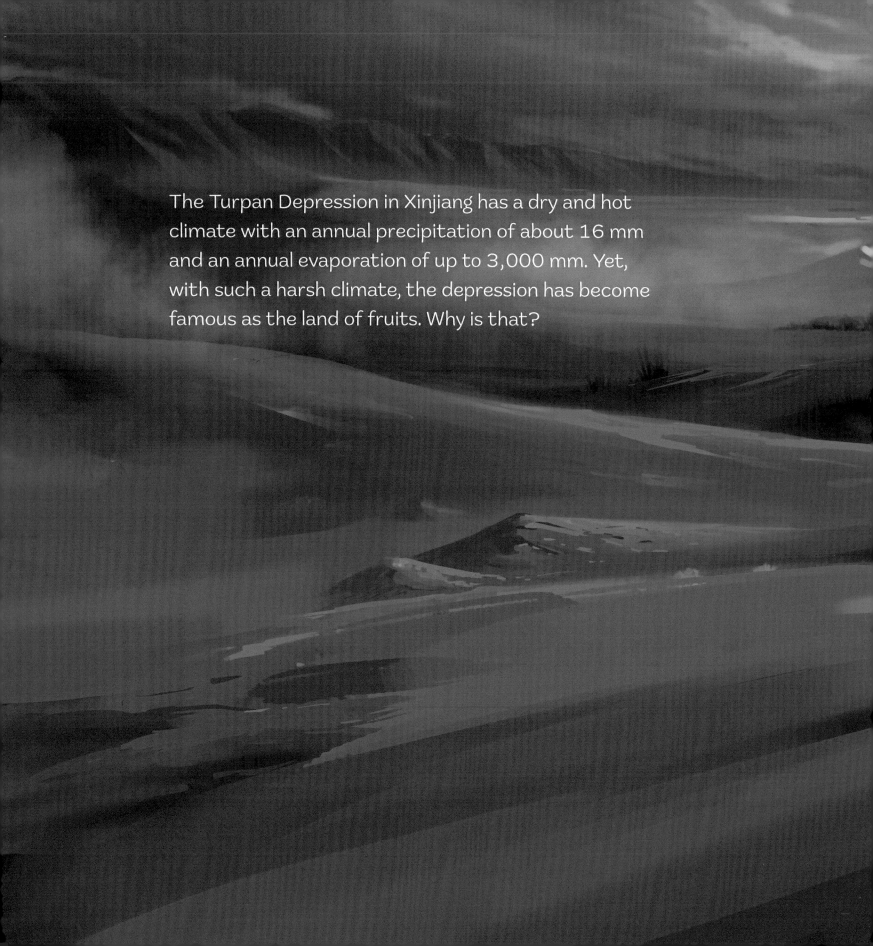

The Turpan Depression in Xinjiang has a dry and hot climate with an annual precipitation of about 16 mm and an annual evaporation of up to 3,000 mm. Yet, with such a harsh climate, the depression has become famous as the land of fruits. Why is that?

The mystery lies in Tianshan (Celestial Mountain in Chinese), which stretches across the Xinjiang region. Due to its lofty terrain, snow accumulates on the summit of Tianshan all year round. When the snow melts in the summer, it provides the depression with abundant water sources.

But these water sources have high seasonality as they are melted from snow water. In summer, when large amounts of snow melt, summer floods occur. People will be exposed to danger if they live too close to the mountain. But if they live too far, melted snow water gradually disappears before reaching them due to evaporation and seepage.

People started to try different methods to access the water source, but none were effective. They may not reach the water source if they drill wells in the desert area. Even if people did open up a water source, the problem of "dry well" occur during autumn and winter. The source of domestic water for Turpan people thus could not be guaranteed.

If people build an outdoor artificial canal and directly connect it to higher places, problems like flow cutoff in winter and evaporation in summer will happen.

During the Han Dynasty, Emperor Wu founded a new county in Xinjiang for migration to manage the Hexi Corridor better. To solve the food supply problem of the local army and residents, Emperor Wu implemented the strategy of military farms. Because there was no water to irrigate the farmland, the local army began to build a large-scale water conservancy project to divert the water of the Luo River for irrigation. Since the bank of the local canal was prone to collapse, the plumbers designed a well for water flowing under it.

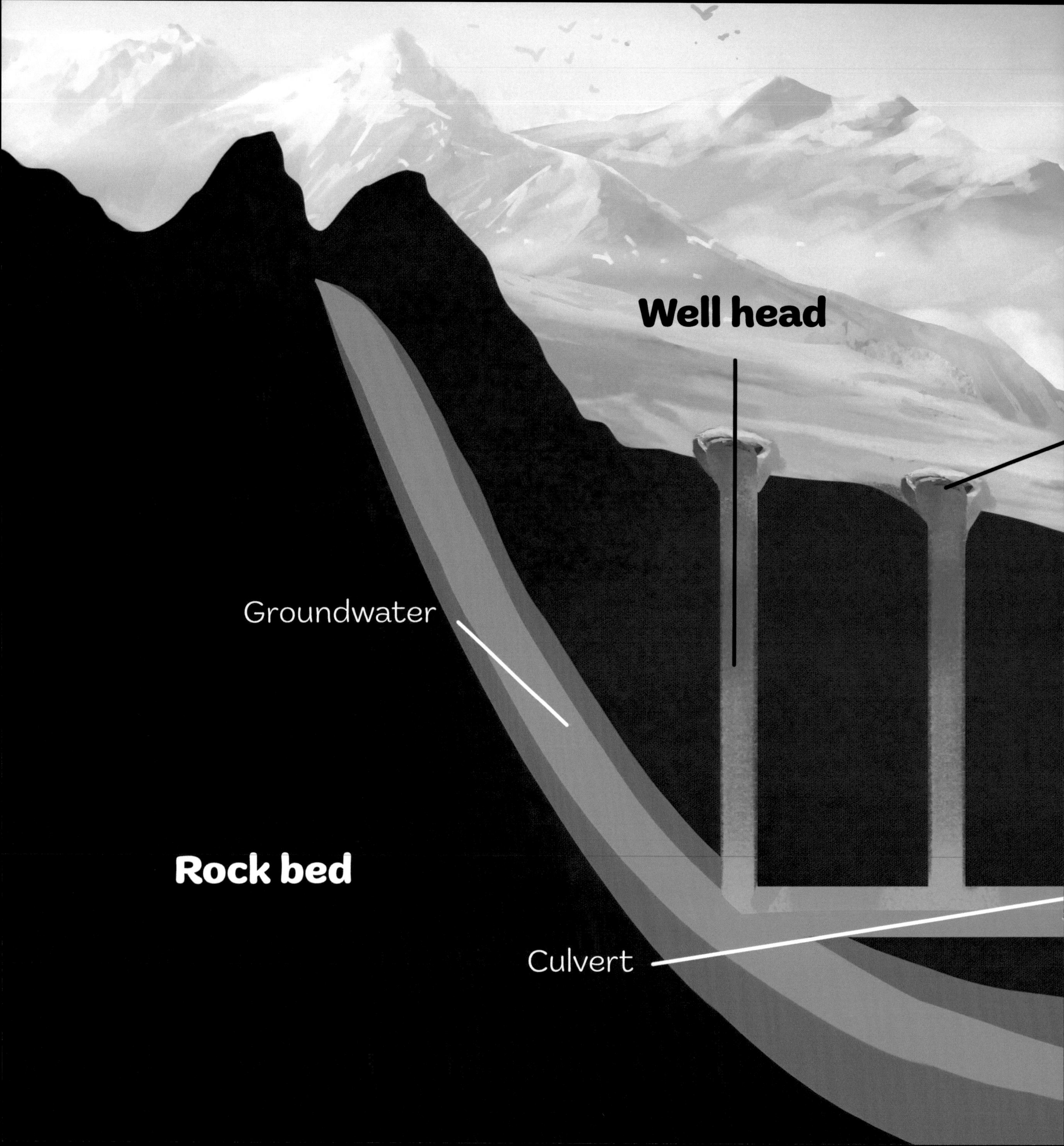
Well head
Groundwater
Rock bed
Culvert

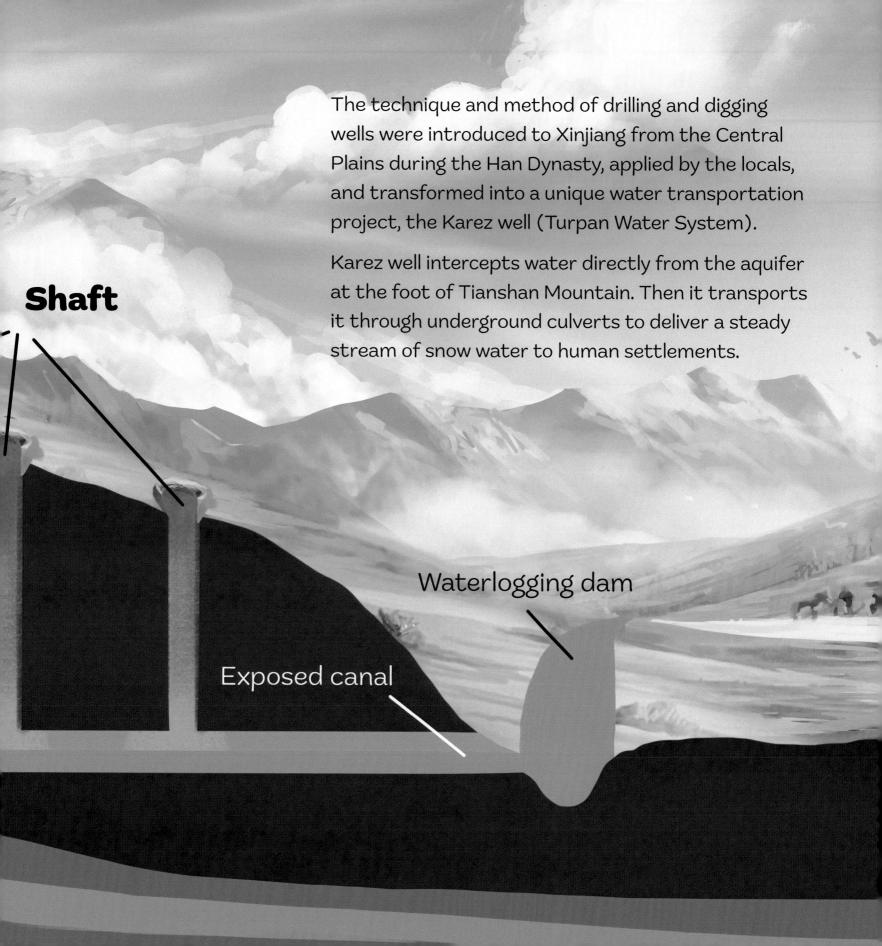

Shaft

The technique and method of drilling and digging wells were introduced to Xinjiang from the Central Plains during the Han Dynasty, applied by the locals, and transformed into a unique water transportation project, the Karez well (Turpan Water System).

Karez well intercepts water directly from the aquifer at the foot of Tianshan Mountain. Then it transports it through underground culverts to deliver a steady stream of snow water to human settlements.

Waterlogging dam

Exposed canal

When we overlook Turpan from the sky, we will notice many holes neatly in the array in the depression. These holes are shafts, a critical component of the Karez well. The main function of shafts is not water intake but the facilitation of gravel transportation, lighting, and ventilation when digging underground culverts.

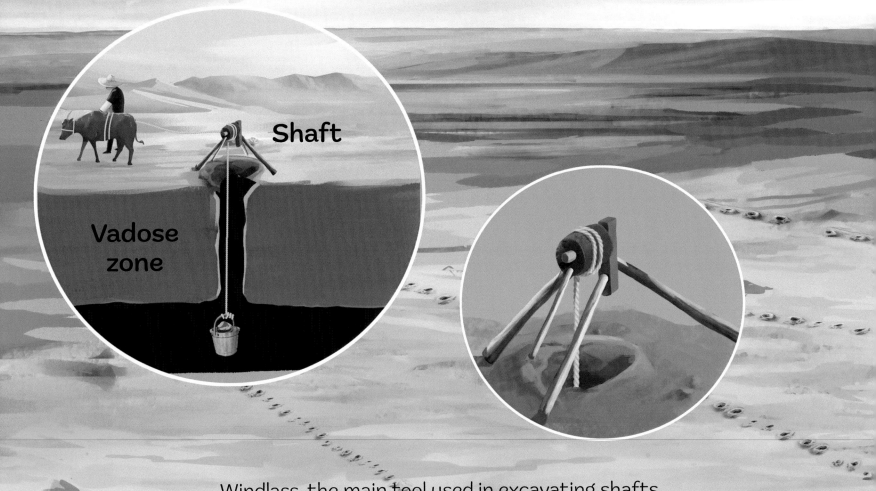

Shaft

Vadose zone

Windlass, the main tool used in excavating shafts, transfers the soil excavated in the shafts and culverts to the ground.

The mound of sand at the wellhead can effectively prevent rainwater and puddle from flowing into Karez well.

When digging the culverts, people first descend to the bottom of the shaft and dig from the bottom of two neighboring shafts towards each other. As shafts are deep down the ground, it is difficult to dig the culvert. To save the maximum amount of labor, culverts normally allow only one person to pass through.

But when people were deep down underground, how did they figure out the direction of excavation of the two neighboring shafts and connect them?

The smart ancients came up with two methods to orient: the wooden stick orientation method and the oil lamp orientation method.

The stick orientation method uses a pair of parallel wooden sticks at the head and bottom of two neighboring shafts. As long as the two sticks at the wellhead are in one straight line, the two shafts can be connected by digging toward the direction of the sticks at the bottom of the well.

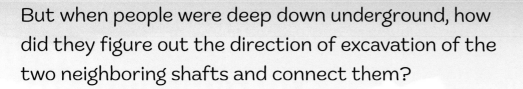

Stick orientation method

Oil lamp orientation method

The oil lamp orientation method uses a burning oil lamp at the bottom of the well. As long as people make sure that they remain in one straight line with their shadow when digging back against the oil lamp, two shafts can then be connected.

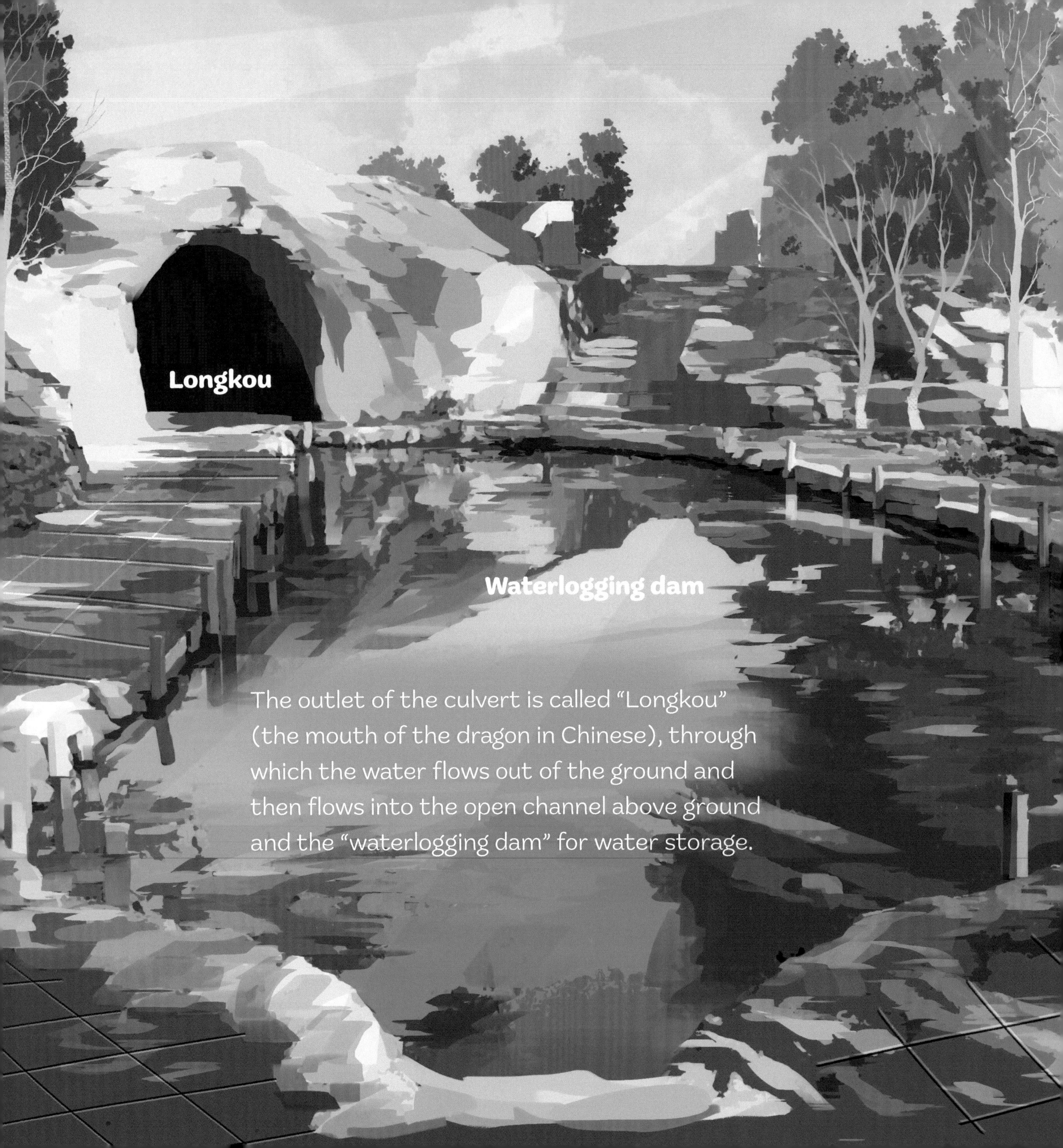

Longkou

Waterlogging dam

The outlet of the culvert is called "Longkou" (the mouth of the dragon in Chinese), through which the water flows out of the ground and then flows into the open channel above ground and the "waterlogging dam" for water storage.

Longkou: Longkou is the junction of the open channel and the culvert of the Karez well. It is also the first outlet of the snow water of Tianshan after it permeates through the ground and flows through the culvert to the open channel.

Waterlogging dams: They are pools of different sizes that people built to store and regulate water at certain locations. Water is stored in the flood dam and sent wherever needed.

There are herds of cattle and sheep with high-quality fresh meat.

The grapes of Turpan are world-renowned for diverse varieties. The seedless white grape is called the "Chinese Green Pearl" for its thin skin, tender flesh, and sweet and sour taste.

Karez well provided a constant water source for irrigation and transformed Turpan, which was under an extreme environment, into the "Pearl beyond the Great Wall" with abundant produce.

The Hami melon of Turpan has large fruit, thick and delicate flesh, and a sweet flavor.

The long-staple cotton of Xinjiang is called "The Best Cotton" for its great softness through long and soft fibers and strong warmth due to fast heating speed.

Soon, Karez well was promoted to all regions in Xinjiang. Two figures contributed the most to this process. In 1841, Lin Zexu was demoted to Ili and discovered Karez well while passing through Turpan. He was so impressed that he ordered the improvement and promotion of the technology. As a result, the scale of Karez wells was no longer limited to the central region of the Turpan Depression and expanded to the western area of Toksun County.

The completed canal has turned more than 100,000 mu* of barren land into arable fields and irrigated nearly one-third of the farmlands in the Ili region. In order to commemorate Lin Zexu's achievements, the local people also called Karez well "Lin Gong Well" (Mr. Lin's Well) and the canal "Lin Gong Canal."

* 1 mu = 0.165 acre.

In 1875, Zuo Zongtang was appointed as the Imperial Envoy to supervise and process military affairs in Xinjiang. To guarantee military supplies, he promoted the development of Karez wells by promoting military farms and calling on soldiers and local residents to build water infrastructure, further advancing the development of Karez wells. Under his vigorous promotion, more than 200 new Karez wells were built in Xinjiang, of which the coverage extended to the Hami region and reached the north and south sides of the Tianshan.

Karez well, the great underground water conservancy project, is one of the four major existing ancient projects in China, along with the Great Wall, the Grand Canal, and the Dujiangyan. It is a "Major Historical and Cultural Site Protected at National Level." According to the survey conducted in 1962, there were approximately 1,700 Karez wells in Xinjiang, among which 1,100 are located in Turpan Depression with a total length of about 5 km. Therefore, Karez well was also known as "The Underground Great Wall."

As one of the few "living cultural heritages" on the Silk Road still in use, Karez well has been playing an important role until now. The people of Turpan have also developed a number of Karez well sites for tourists to visit.

However, with the increase in population, the use of agricultural irrigation water, and the development of modern hydraulic technology in recent years, the number of Karez wells in operation has greatly dropped. Most of the Karez wells have dried up and been buried in yellow sand. To undertake the great responsibility of protecting Karez wells, there is still a long way to go.

The significance of the Karez well is much more than that. Before its invention, most areas in Xinjiang lacked water resources. Local residents lived a nomadic lifestyle and settled around water and grass.

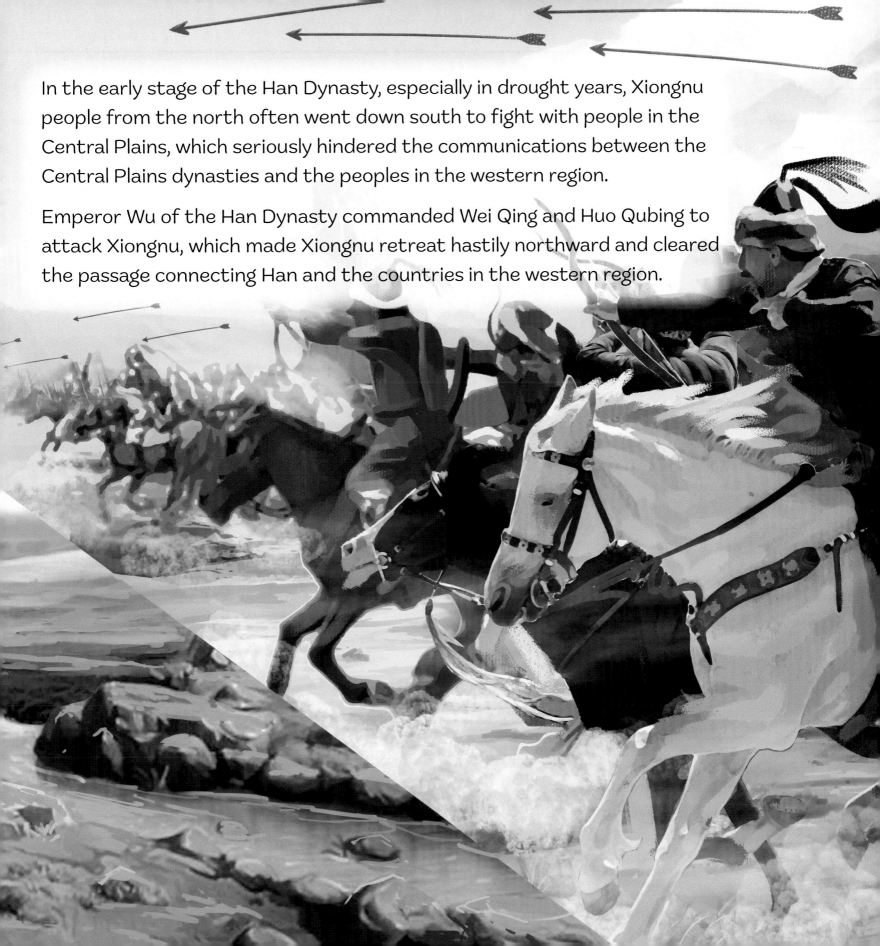

In the early stage of the Han Dynasty, especially in drought years, Xiongnu people from the north often went down south to fight with people in the Central Plains, which seriously hindered the communications between the Central Plains dynasties and the peoples in the western region.

Emperor Wu of the Han Dynasty commanded Wei Qing and Huo Qubing to attack Xiongnu, which made Xiongnu retreat hastily northward and cleared the passage connecting Han and the countries in the western region.

During the period of Emperor Xuan of the Han Dynasty, the Protectorate of Western Regions was set up to supervise Xinjiang, which marked the official jurisdiction of Xinjiang as a part of the Han Dynasty. Due to the earlier opening of the Silk Road by Zhang Qian, Xinjiang has become a strategic pass for communications between the East and the West. Thanks to the nourishment of the water from Karez wells, there was a stable food supply. People also settled, forming towns where merchants from the East and West stopped off for trading.

Karez wells irrigated farmlands and transformed nomadic civilization into agrarian civilization. It enables local residents to live a peaceful and happy life and improves the stability of the borderland, leading to long-lasting peace in the country.

Chinese Pioneering Inventions Series

Karez Well

Edited by Li Chaodong
Translated by Xuemeng Angela Li

First published in 2023 by Royal Collins Publishing Group Inc.
Groupe Publication Royal Collins Inc.
BKM Royalcollins Publishers Private Limited

Headquarters: 550-555 boul. René-Lévesque O Montréal (Québec) H2Z1B1 Canada
India office: 805 Hemkunt House, 8th Floor, Rajendra Place, New Delhi 110 008

Original Edition © Hohai University Press

ISBN: 978-1-4878-1103-7

To find out more about our publications, please visit www.royalcollins.com.

About the Editor

Li Chaodong, born in 1963, graduated from the Department of History of East China Normal University. He is a famous education publisher in China. He has edited and published more than 50 sets of books. He has won the title of "National Leading Talent in Press and Publication" and "China's Annual Publication Figure." He is the Founding Vice President of the All-China Federation of Industry and Commerce Book Industry Chamber of Commerce, Vice President of the Fifth Council of China Book Publishing Association, Vice Chairman of Anhui Publishing Association, and Vice Chairman of Jiangsu Publishing Association.